LIONEL AGGETT'S

ANDALUCÍA & LAS ALPUJARRAS

An Artist in Lemon Country

HALSGROVE
In association with

THE
JOHN DAVIES
GALLERY

First published in Great Britain in 2002

British Library Cataloguing-in-Publication Data
A CIP record for this title is available from the British Library

ISBN 1 84114 195 X

HALSGROVE

Halsgrove House
Lower Moor Way
Tiverton, Devon EX16 6SS
Tel: 01884 243242
Fax: 01884 243325
email: sales@halsgrove.com
website: www.halsgrove.com

Printed and bound in Italy by
Centro Grafico Ambrosiano

CONTENTS

Montilla, Córdoba.
pastel, 500x650mm

ACKNOWLEDGEMENTS AND DEDICATIONS

I would like to thank John Davies for hosting the solo exhibitions of my Spanish paintings, notably 'A Spanish Daybook' and 'Lionel Aggett In Lemon Country', many of which appear in this book, through the kind courtesy of their owners.

My thanks to Kostka and Lucy Garcia-Miñaur for translating Monola's two songs, and to John Brough of Andalucían Adventures (for whom Lucy works, and I have tutored), for introducing me to the beautiful Sierras Subbéticas. Also to Carbos and José for their excellent hospitality at the Hotel Zuhayra, Zuheros, our only stay throughout Spain, not under canvas.

Thanks to John Melville, photographer, for his excellent transparencies, also to Jane Henderson of the Gilders Workshop for framing my shows so superbly, and to my brother Reginald for his meticulous framing and mount cutting.

This book is dedicated to my darling wife Anne, our son Russell, his wife Lynn and their daughter Lucy, our daughter Kate, her husband Trevor, and their children Lily and George. Also Dustin our faithful tabby, and to Sennen our characterful Siamese, both a huge inspiration to my fellow artist Anne.

Lionel Aggett, September 2002

Market, Orgiva, Las Alpujarras, Granada.
Diary 29 May 1997

FOREWORD

I met Lionel and his wife Anne in 1995, and his first one-man show at Stow-on-the-Wold was staged in 1996. This exhibition, titled *At Home and Abroad*, featured scenes from Devon, Cornwall and the Cotswolds, as well as from France and Italy.

Because of its wide terms of reference, it was an ideal first exhibition to introduce Lionel's work at Stow, and the response, as I had anticipated, was extremely enthusiastic. Very much the travelling artist, his four subsequent one-man shows at the gallery, well planned in advance, have all been based on one particular route on the continent.

In 1997, a journey through Spain inspired by Laurie Lee's *As I Walked Out One Summer Morning* resulted in the strong and well received *A Spanish Daybook* which so effectively revealed this hot and rugged country. Two years later Lionel produced a number of wonderfully contrasting images in *Great Rivers of France*, from the flowing placidity of the Seine, the pools of Giverny, the Canal du Berry, the serene vistas of the Loire to the dramatic gorges of the Dordogne and the Lot. During the first year in the new millennium he returned to Spain, and concentrated on Andalucía and Las Alpujarras for the exhibition *In Lemon Country*. In this show Lionel included a memorable body of work featuring some of the majestic valleys in the foothills of the Sierra Nevada, together with some magnificent views in La Mancha and Córdoba.

In 2003 the John Davies Gallery is looking forward to hosting his fifth one-man show, which will reveal his coast-to-coast encounters in Italy, from Amalfi north through Umbria and Tuscany, and onwards to include Venice. Lionel also intends including a group of his fresh and spontaneous watercolours of the Cotswolds.

One of the most entertaining aspects of preparing the catalogues for Lionel's exhibitions is that of reading his daybooks. Generally on each expedition he fills two or three cloth-bound sketchhooks with drawings, watercolour studies and extensive written notes of his encounters. These provide an intimate insight into his approach, and are a joy to handle, not only for their texture, but also for the freshness of the watercolour work. In addition, one cannot fail to be engaged by his infectious enthusiasm for the sights that inspire him – the scenes themselves, their character, the light, the flora and fauna – very little escapes the attention and curiosity of this enthusiastic communicator.

His journals also reveal his lively interest in the produce of each region he visits. Lionel has a preference for quite mature VW camper vans and has often been accompanied on his working trips by his wife, Anne. Wine is purchased from local vineyards and food from markets whenever possible, so much so that the couple would certainly be capable of produchig an authoritative guide to French, Italian and Spanish regional fare!

Nevertheless, the lighter side never interrupts the work ethic, and Lionel will almost always be up to catch the early light sketching, watercolour drawing or even working direct on site in his preferred medium of pastel; similarly he can be still outside at the end of a long day, catching the evening light. This approach, together with his well-honed skills as a draughtsman, gives his work great authenticity. These attributes, together with his highly developed pastel technique, distinguish him as a very fine topographical landscape artist.

John Davies
The John Davies Gallery
June 2002

Barrio Troglodita, Santiago, Guadix.
Diary 25 May 1997

INTRODUCTION

The village, affectionately known to locals as 'el pescado' on account of its resemblance to a fish when viewed from above, lies dormant, stretched out below us. The chill of the mountain air which threatened to penetrate our trusty VW camper parked on the terrace high above the rooftops is already being tempered by the first rays of sunlight appearing from behind the base of the Cerro de los Murciélago towering above us. The east-facing roof slopes glint like scales as the sunrise gathers pace, gradually illuminating the distant pillars of smoke rising vertically into the still air from the burning mounds of olive cuttings. The refrain of an Andalucían copla, followed immediately by another, drifts upwards through the empty alleys and narrow streets :

> Volando voy, volando vengo
> Volando voy, volando vengo
> por el camino me entretengo
>
> Enamorao de la vida
> Aunque a veces duela
> Si tengo frio, busco candela
>
> I fly here, I fly there
> I fly here, I fly there
> I amuse myself along the way
>
> In love with life
> Although sometimes it hurts
> If I'm cold I look for a flame

Then nearer and louder, the words ringing as clear as a bell :

> Ay luna que brilla en los mares
> Los mares oscuros
> Ay luna tu no estas cansada
> De girar al mismo mundo?
>
> Oh moon, that shines in the seas
> The dark seas
> Oh moon aren't you tired
> Of circling the same world?

Monola, one of the village's best loved and respected characters, is returning form the groves, the fragrance of the bruised and scorched olive wood preceding him, as evidence of his early endeavours; his morning's work done, the rest of the village beginning to stir.

Zuheros is located in the Sierras Subbéticas south of Córdoba. The tight cluster of white houses tumbles down the hill below the romantic Moorish castle on a rocky outcrop beneath the north face of the mountain towering behind, and surrounded on three sides by olive groves. It is a perfect example of the unspoiled Andalucían hill village which epitomises the rural charm of inland Spain.

Market, Orgiva, Las Alpujarras, Granada.
Diary 29 May 1997

Landscape near Zagrilla, Sierras Subbéticas, Córdoba.   pastel, 400x500mm

Springtime in Andalucía is a joy. The clear air intensifies the bright rich colours of new growth, and the scent released by the numerous wild flowers and leaves springing from bud, heightens the senses. Verdant patches, later turning burnt-sienna dry, contrast with vivid splashes of blood-red poppies, intermingled with violet blues, purple pinks and yellows. The myriad of colour is extended further by the rich earth colours running from reds, burnt siennas through to umbers and ochres to an almost blinding white.

Warm foreground colours and strong tonal contrasts gradually become cooler into the middle distance with the tonal extremes merging, until violet-blue accents take the eye to the far horizon guided by the perspective of seemingly endless brigades of marching olives. The clear vibrant light is manifested in the sunlit buildings, and the strong shadows cast by the olives, their dark trunks contrasting with blue-tinged olive-green foliage, and silver-grey-tipped highlights shimmering where leaves are turned by the strengthening breeze.

HOME BASE AND TRAVEL

I draw much of my inspiration from my local landscape, and heritage, and have for the most of my life painted the beautiful and varied scenery of Devon and Cornwall. The challenge of capturing the moment, atmosphere, light and character at a particular locality/region fascinates me. Light is constantly on the turn, thus changing the physiognomy of the landscape through from dawn 'till dusk, and is further influenced by climatic and regional differences. Nowhere is this more apparent than when painting deep into Dartmoor when suddenly the infamous mist can descend and then block out the scene completely. Compass to the fore!

Dartmoor and Exmoor, are quite different; one rugged and the other softer and rounder. South, North, East and West Devon all present varied landscapes, and some of the most intricately patterned and undulating are on my back doorstep: the rich Devon Red farmlands of Mid-Devon rolling across from the north edge of eastern Dartmoor to the Exe Valley. Whilst the light here is muted and soft, the West Penwith of Cornwall is conversely illuminated with intense vibrancy, the light bouncing off the sea on all three sides of the peninsula.

Why then, with all this material within one's grasp, is there the need to travel? I have enjoyed the feeling of 'adventure' from my early student days; study trips to Italy in the late-fifties, an R.I.B.A. scholarship trip to Venice in 1959 on a 1956, 150cc Lambretta with my pal and fellow student David Rhys riding pillion! A further R.I.B.A. scholarship stay in Rome at the Rome School in 1962 paved the way for future painting expeditions in Europe. The thrill of experiencing new locations and conditions fires all inspirational instincts and tests the resolve of a landscape painter. Exploring new horizons broadens and develops the ability to respond to widely different situations and subject matter. The vastly improved modes of travel available today, compared with my own early 'modest' excursions have opened up far wider and distant horizons for exploration. Today's student back-packers would probably view my early excitement at hiking in Norway and so forth with disdain! So far, however, the enjoyment, convenience and complete independence enjoyed and sustained through the use of our 'travelling studio' has restricted our adventures to Europe. It is not perhaps for everyone, and there is maybe something to be said for sticking to one subject. It is a personal thing, which seems to work for me. As well as differences there are similarities; for instance, the field patterns, undulation and perspective of crops, to be found in Tuscany, Umbria and Piedmont are similar to those which exist in my native Devon. The light there, however, is different but not so vibrant as that to be experienced in Provence or Almeria.

Headland Warren, Dartmoor.
pastel, 250x325mm

Mid-Devon Landscape (Exe Valley).
pastel, 250x325mm

Golden Harvest, Paul, Cornwall.
pastel, 250x325mm

I have also explored the many regions of France and here, too, each area displays its own particular character and mood forged by the topography, climate, culture and occupation of its people. Normandy, Brittany, the Dordogne, Berry and Provence, to name but a few, are all quite different. As with many other artists, Provence draws me back time after time, to experience and capture the vibrant shimmering light and varied landscape, supporting settlements which appear to be hewn out of the very rock upon which they have grown.

Following an early visit with the family to the Basque area both sides of the border between France and Spain in the 1970s, I was inspired to probe deeper into rural Spain by the writings of Laurie Lee who was a distant relative of my wife, Anne. Her mother, née Wilson, was a Lee from Stroud in Gloucester. My solo trip in 1997 was loosely based on his epic journey on foot, and beautifully documented in his book *As I Walked Out One Midsummer's Morning*. Some of my sketches and paintings from this particular trip are reproduced in the following pages along with those executed during our working visit in 2001.

Gerald Brenan's *South of Granada* records his experiences as an inhabitant at Yegen in Las Alpujarras, and if you intend to visit this unique part of Andalucía you will find his book an inspirational read. So, too, is Chris Stewart's more recent best seller *Driving Over Lemons*, a marvellous account of his family's experience at starting a new life, in the Guadalfeo Valley near Orgiva, and now followed by his sequel *A Parrot in the Pepper Tree*. Chris also acts as a guide to walking parties organised by Andalucían Adventures, and for whom I have also tutored at Zuheros.

There is a feast of material in this wondrous and spacious land of illusions. In the crisp clear air of La Mancha the windmills at Consuegra seem close enough to touch, and practically every journey undertaken is longer than it seems on the map. Such is the joy of travelling in our VW camper van and tent, following one's nose, the journey roughly planned, but open to any diversion where the ever-changing landscape beckons, punctuated by the irresistible hill villages or isolated cortijos, all illuminated by the hot sun and set against varied backdrops of vineyards, olive groves or endless carpets of ripening cereals.

I may be stating the obvious, but prior to every working trip undertaken, I spend the previous winter reading and researching new areas, familiarising myself with local topography and orientation etc. This saves time when travelling. Nevertheless, much of what I do is spontaneous often deviating from even the sketchiest of plans. It is a good discipline to work within some sort of overall structure though, which will then facilitate the numerous diversions inspired by creative needs.

Our camper van is a real workhorse. The model, an Auto-Sleeper Trooper, our preferred choice, has the facility of a well-designed rising roof, enabling the vehicle to be used as a 'transporter' for delivering paintings to galleries in the UK and, with good storage, doubles as a travelling studio with on-board accommodation for working trips. We also take a tent which acts as a base at our principal destinations, whereas we sleep on board when in travelling mode. Unlike the larger campers, the standard wheel-base enables us to gain access to narrow tracks and therefore interesting and unusual locations.

Location shot with VW.

Painting of Olvera in progress.

Working below the Puente Nuevo Ronda.

APPROACH

The crisp crunch of the pastel across a textured surface, whether delivered with the flat face or inclined point, excites me every time a new painting is started. The manipulative twist of the pastel held between finger tips rotated with increased pressure to create a sharp edge against softer feathered passages is a thrilling part of the 'pure' pastel technique to execute.

The manner in which such strokes are made contributes to each artist's individual style. It is a joy I first experienced in 1968 when we were living in Truro, Cornwall. I had painted mostly in oils, acrylics and watercolour until then. Over the years I have experimented with and developed my approach to painting.

During the late '70s and '80s I courted a 'hard line' semi-abstract approach based on field studies, and in tandem with plein air work. I used mixed media too, a combination of pastel, gouache, watercolour and acrylic. I have for some years now, however, concentrated on pastel in its purest form, unadulterated by other materials, using various supports. Although much striking work is currently produced using a combination of different materials, pastel is, for me, seen at its best when used alone to achieve the myriad of effects, of which it is extremely capable.

Rich saturated and unsaturated colour with deep tonal contrasts through to the subtlest of exchanges achieved by the lightest of touches can be expressed through the wonderfully velvet texture which the medium possesses. The strokes can convey the artist's response to mood and atmosphere in a very individual and recognisable way, similar to brush or knife marks, and indeed handwriting.

My method of working is based on my preference for working directly from nature. I feel there is no greater painterly challenge than to set up, whatever the elements determine to throw at you, and paint on the spot. There can be all sorts of distractions ranging from wind, rain, the unexpected lorry parked in front of you when half an hour into your painting, the odd inquisitive onlooker who refuses to stop talking, or simply a large battery of people – an audience no less! In the middle of Dartmoor one can avoid the latter, but not in the Campo, Siena, nor in the Mirador S. Nicolas, Granada!

You have to aim for a particular moment in the day's cycle, for the sun, and therefore the light, which together with the weather conditions, determines the mood and atmosphere, is constantly on the turn. Observations have to be made, and at the same time you must 'carry' the chosen moment as you work to capture the atmosphere.

Sometimes the painting is completed in my studio, and occasionally I will just establish tonal differences on site, and then work on the subject later in the studio. Another solution is to revisit the site at the same period each day as Monet did.

I also sketch on site, taking notes, and sometimes using watercolour as a reference for a painting to be produced later in the studio. Here I find the experience of plein air work assists in transporting a painterly approach to the studio. Much of painting is derived from intense observation, and when accompanied by the briefest of sketches can form the basis for a work of great complexity in terms of mood and atmosphere. The method of which Turner was the master.

My eyesight enables me to see clearly over long distances (I wear bi-focals for reading) and this, I am sure, influences the way I observe the landscape. My eyes explore the middle and far horizon, highlighting points of interest: the warm light on distant buildings, their sunlit gable ends contrasting with the landscape, which gradually turns from the warmth of the foreground to the cooler distant blue hues as my eyes explore further out. I therefore often enjoy the wider expansive view, observed, following a hike with rucksack laden with pastels etc. up the side of some crag or other. Such a subject can, through a combination of linear perspective, tonal variation and pictorial perspective, together with compositional and pivotal elements, engage and hold the eye.

I feel that a landscape painting should leave the onlooker with no doubts as to where, when and under what conditions it was painted. The palette/mix should convey the region and, through the handling of the light conditions, the season and time of day. The artist's feelings, response and reason for painting a particular view will communicate through his or her expression of the mood and

Pigments, pastels, and a selection from the Unison range

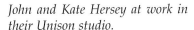

John and Kate Hersey at work in their Unison studio.

atmosphere, a quality far beyond and at a different level to general expertise and competence in technique.

The work featured in this book is either in pastel or watercolour, two media that are ideal to use when travelling. The pastels are packed in a portfolio, each secured with tape at all four corners with a sheet of newspaper cut slightly larger and secured in the same manner.

I have used Unison Pastels for the last fourteen years, and first made contact with John and Kate Hersey in 1988 not long after they started their highly successful business at Tarset in Northumberland. Their pastels are very well known now, and deservedly so. The range is the result of much painstaking research into the structure and unity of colour. As John says, 'The colours are considered as imitating the sun itself. As lovers of the sun, just as moths are. The sun is everywhere in the colour but the colour is never stable and can never be. It is always on the turn whilst tied to the invisible sun, hence its beauty.'

The system has been developed and enlarged since then, but the principle behind the structure remains the same. The range is not made up, as is usually the case, by the mechanical addition of either black or white, a process which results in a whole series of stepped reductions or tints, having no reference to the whole. Each colour is available in a set of 18 (some 36) harmonic blends. They are instead grouped in pairs as a movement around a centre of intense sunlight and can be seen as separate colours, and as a unity, a unison. The pastels are numbered for re-ordering. The shades of each colour i.e. blue-violet, green, brown-earth, etc. relate to one another with regard to both their position and numbering in each box. I find their system to be completely in sympathy with my way of working, and I have an empathy with their fascination over the influence that the ever-changing light has on the mood and atmosphere of each and every subject.

I have experimented with various textured surfaces, pastel papers, tinted watercolour papers and coated boards. I currently favour pastel card, a stout card with an application of cork particles tinted in several colours. Although the finish is easily damaged by water, it is extremely suitable for pure soft pastel work. The surface is kinder to the fingertips than glass paper, and holds a lot of pastel. The texture receives both vigorous and subtle feathered strokes and expresses a painterly approach very well.

There are several paintings of the Las Alpujarras region later in the book. One of my favourite haunts overlooks the Poqueira Ravine, a view which I have both painted and sketched. When not painting on the spot I use site sketches to produce a painting later in the studio. I always keep an illustrated working diary, recorded each day during my painting trips. Drawings or watercolours awash with freely applied paint, often with colour notes, are spread across one or two leaves of my home-made sketch book. I then write diary and further painting notes around the image at the end of each day. This is both an extremely valuable tool for studio work on my return, and a detailed personal account of the journey.

The sketch of Bubión and Capileira (below) was made on 27 May 2001 during my working trip in preparation for the one-person exhibition in November 2001 at the John Davies Gallery, Stow-on-the-Wold, Gloucestershire. The form of the two upper villages running obliquely from left to right, up and across the picture plane is a classic composition. The eye is taken into the painting along the lines of trees up through the villages to the Veleta peak towering above. The larger painting of the same view, shown on page 113, was completed wholly on location in 1997.

LA painting on site overlooking the Poqueira Ravine.

Bubión and Capileira, Granada.
Diary 27 May 2001

Bubión and Capileira, Las Alpujarras, Granada.
pastel, 500x400mm

The studio painting executed using the diary sketch, together with a catalogued record of the previous painting.

One of my many excursions whilst staying in Granada was to the Sierra de la Parapanda and the village of Montefrío in the western reaches of the province. The impressively-sited white-washed houses sit gracefully on two hills, one of which is curiously shaped like a hog's back. Set amongst a sea of olives, the views towards the village are characterised by the complex multi point perspective of the groves, seemingly marching over the contours on collision courses! The painting (below) is an example of my plein air work, completed on site in 1997, and unusually the view was not the reward for a long hike. Our former VW (right) was parked just off the road with the sliding door conveniently facing towards Montefrío so that if caught by the odd shower or two I could have worked from inside the van. The need did not fortunately arise!

The eye is encouraged to explore right into the picture, from the warm foreground along the lines of olives and tracks, punctuated here and there by cortijos, to the village and cooler hues beyond. The haze imparts a sense of mystery and grandeur, and the understated periphery of the work accentuates the impressive location of the village, as does the composition.

Montefrío, Sierra de la Parapanda, Granada.
pastel, 500x650mm

The picture below is a free and 'painterly' rendering of what is for me a most unforgettable and dramatic view of Ronda from the south, completed wholly on the spot (left). The locals use the track leading to the Iglesia Rupestre de la Virgen de la Cabeza, a small ninth-century Mozarabic monastery, as part of their circular 'constitutional' walk. During all the times I have painted along the dusty lane, I have seen only a few tourists. In spring it is quiet, apart from the birdsong, and if you are lucky (for they are soon cut), the olives are surrounded by vivid and dense splashes of poppies.

Vigorous strokes from the flat surface of my pastels are used to convey the drama before me. There is an economy of touch, contrasted with the impression of detail in the town perched high above the ravine of the Guadalevin river. Crisp, firm applications of the pastel indicate the sunlit faces of buildings whilst much of the 'ground' is left untouched in the foreground, middle distance and cliff face.

Ronda from Track, Malaga.
pastel, 500x650mm

Alhambra, Granada.
Diary 24 May 2001

Occasionally I will paint using a combination of sketches to produce a 'constructed' work, i.e. a sunset where observation supplemented by brief sketches is the best way of recording a rapidly changing lighting effect.

The view from the Mirador de San Nicolás of the ochre coloured walls of the Alhambra, intensified under the warm glow of the setting sun is one of the most breathtaking in Granada, and probably the world. Compared with the location outside Ronda, the painter has plenty of company here. If you do not mind working in front of a crowd, this particular experience is one not to be missed. As well as producing the sketches (and others) illustrated, I spent an evening or two just looking, for the glorious effect of the lowering sun on this mighty edifice changes constantly.

The watercolour records the whole composition, and the smaller study a period prior to the warmest glow. The effect is never quite the same, and particularly at springtime some visitors are unlucky to catch a cloudy evening. One such couple next to us at the campsite in 2001 only had one chance before moving on and cloud cover appeared just as the drama began to unfold!

Sunset.   Diary 28 May 1997

The Alhambra Sunset, Granada.
pastel, 500x400mm
A studio painting executed from the sketches illustrated opposite.

JOURNEY TO ANDALUCÍA

It is a wonderful feeling of freedom, heading down the A38, the VW stocked with painting materials, and our additional accommodation, i.e. tent, together with items deemed necessary for a six-week venture. Provisions are included for the first two or three days before we buy fresh produce from the local markets. We 'set sail' from Plymouth at 8am on the day/night crossing scheduled to arrive at Santander at 9.30am the following day. The working diary commences from day one, and there are plenty of subjects on board enabling me to loosen up and get started.

The sea can be very rough in the Bay of Biscay but I have only experienced one storm and that was at night. Conditions were still grim on arrival at Santander and we disembarked in a torrential downpour. The situation was made even worse, for when waved on by a steward, I neatly removed the vent from the roof when it failed to clear a sprinkler! Apologies from all quarters as crewmen frantically set about plugging the hole with a large plastic bag and Scotch tape. This 'repair' lasted during gradually improving conditions until I reached the plain beyond Burgos when it was dispatched by the wind. I pulled off the N1.E5 into Gumiel de Hizán, a small village where I purchased a strong pvc sheet and insulation tape. Watched by a group of fascinated locals short of entertainment, I clambered on top of the van and made the repair. It lasted the entire trip!

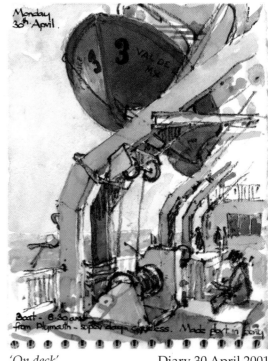

'On deck'.   Diary 30 April 2001

On arrival Anne and I are greeted by the beautiful sight of Santander, sparkling under a clear blue sky against the backcloth of the snow-covered Cordillera Cantabrica. This range, incorporating the Picos de Europa to the west, is a dramatic introduction to the Iberian Peninsula with a long climb up to the land of El Cid, high on the plateau of Castilla Y León and the Duero basin, at about 1000m (3300ft).

Laurie Lee walked from Vigo on the west coast, eastwards to Valladolid in this area, during July 1935, and every time I arrive in the vast splendour of inland Spain I wonder at the achievement of his epic journey on foot down through Spain in the searing heat of high summer. Indeed he suffered sunstroke and hallucinations before he reached Valladolid. We follow his route from Segovia through Toledo, Valdepeñas, Córdoba and Seville down to Jerez. Whereas he walked around the coast from Cadiz as far as Castillo and Altofaro, we travel eastwards from Jerez through inland Andalucía.

How things must have changed since 1935, and again following the post civil war and Franco years. The effects of nearly forty years under a regime intent on suppressing the cultural and intellectual aspirations of its people who produced excellent artists, musicians, poets, writers and film directors, have been all but obliterated by the incredible speed with which Spain is recovering her role as one of Europe's most culturally inspired countries. Social, political and cultural reforms have been implemented and accepted, and democracy has been such an inspirational success that Franco, who died in 1975, is almost forgotten.

The 500th Anniversary of Colombus's voyage to the New World, Expo and the Barcelona Olympics, all in 1992, helped to kick start the regeneration of infrastructure and communications. The roads have been steadily improving, and I have noticed a difference even over the last six years. Whereas, in our 1982 VW, I was reduced to 10 mph along some stretches in Andalucía, the roads are now excellently surfaced.

The N1.E5 highway from Burgos towards Madrid is good, and if you are not touring this area, and are heading south as we are, it facilitates a swift advance, even for a camper van. For this reason we have yet to stop at Burgos beyond which lies the vast sparsely-populated plateau of the Duero, with only the occasional village breaking the endless horizon. Eventually the Cordillera Ilberica (to the east) and Cordillera Central (to the south) form distant violet-blue backdrops.

During spring the weather conditions can worsen as the road nears the base of the Sierra de Guadarrama, which together with the Sierra de Gredos forms the Cordillera Central. On 1 May 2001 we encountered a blinding snow storm as we left the N1.E5 at La Pinilla and headed southwest for Segovia along the northern side of the Sierra. We were forced to stop as the visibility was down to practically zero under the leadened sky, and the snow ploughs which seemed to appear from nowhere busy keeping the route open. The snow did not settle for long and by the time we eventually arrived in Segovia most had gone. There were still remnants clinging to roofs with menacing snow clouds overhead, as the sketch below from the Altos de Fuencisla shows. The van's heater was used that evening, and snow still lay on the lower slopes to the west of the campsite the following morning!

Segovia is worthy of a longer stay, which we did on our return journey that year. There are superb cameos everywhere, and townscape

Segovia, Castilla Y León.   Diary 4 June 2001

subjects abound. The street architecture is renowned for its golden-coloured masonry and plaster façades with Mudéjar geometrical designs or esgrafiados. The golden-ochre stone when viewed across this cornfield on our return in June, seemed an extension of nature, contrasting delightfully with the violet-blue backcloth of the Sierra de Guadarrama behind.

Segovia, Castilla Y León.
Diary 1 May 2001

If you stay at the campsite just outside Segovia, it is advisable to catch the bus into town for the day, as parking can be difficult. The bus leaves from a side road opposite. We alighted at the cathedral in the centre and returned from the aqueduct. The old town or Ciudad Vieja is circled by ramparts and is perched on a triangular rock at an altitude of 1000m (3300ft) hence the likelihood of snow in early spring. The site is quite extraordinary, and is dominated by the cathedral roughly in the centre, towering over the delightful Plaza Major, with the Alcazar to the northwest and the Acueducto Romano to the southeast.

A sketch of the Plaza Major looking across to the cathedral from our table after a 'snack' lunch was followed by the watercolour sketch (right) looking down the Calle Daoiz Marqués del Arco beside the cathedral on the left. The lovely ochre stone is much in evidence and greatly enhances the strong turret form of the cathedral building with its pivotal accent adding character to the street. There was much interest from both locals and tourists including two shop owners who came across at five-minute intervals to discuss my progress! Most amusing of all was when, in response to a tap on my shoulder, I turned around, making a loud Goon-like exclamation – thinking it was Anne returning from her shopping expedition – to be confronted with five nuns, one of whom tapped her temple and with a kindly smile said 'Bueno'. At least I think that was what she said!

Incidentally, I am sometimes asked how long the sketches take. It really depends on the complexity of the subject and, however complicated, my response to it. Generally they take a quarter to three-quarters of an hour. This one took approximately half an hour. When on the road, they are usually executed during coffee, lunch or tea stops, and during working days, almost at any time, in support of a full painting or instead of! Sometimes I will spend a whole day searching and recording subjects.

The painting opposite, of the city from the eastern side, was painted in the studio from studies made on 7 May 1997. This is perhaps the most dramatic view showing the Roman aqueduct as well as the old town. A loose approach with warm colours through to hazy blues provides depth and mood. The diary sketch will some day be used for a painting.

Calle Daoiz Marqués del Arco, Segovia, Castilla Y León.
Diary 5 June 2001

Calle Daoiz Marqués
del Arco.
Segovia.

decorative lines of the pillars and ribs in the vaulting, to make the interior both light and elegant. The organ music (unfortunately piped) added to the atmosphere, somehow increasing the elevation!
We made our way from the cathedral, & across the Plaza Mayor looking for a suitable restaurant for a medium/light lunch & which would afford an interesting subject to sketch. The result was placed on the previous page! – the food was good!
Fully recharged, we walked to the Alcazar, standing on a cliff overlooking the Eresma valley. The building is resplendent with stucco facades decorated with Mudéjar geometrical designs (esgrafiados) as are most of the buildings in the centre. We continued around the wall and back up to the cathedral where I produced this sketch whilst Anne browsed and did some shopping. The Calle Daoiz Marqués del Arco, running along the north side of the cathedral down to the Alcazar is very characterful, containing many buildings with interesting esgrafiados. The top end, featured in the sketch is lively with shops and people - the entrance to the cathedral is to the left. Crowds of inquisitive onlookers, including some nuns, one of whom tapped me on the shoulder (I made some Goonish reply-thinking it was Anne!) to exclaim the work was bueno. Then a stroll to the aqueduct via the Plaza de San Martín - Commodity, firmness + delight!
Returned to site - pork, tomato, garlic, onion, olive oil/wine vinegar salad + Rioja.

Segovia, Castilla Y León.
pastel, 500x650mm

Further west and on the north side of the Sierra de Gredos, a continuation of the Cordillera Central, lies Avila, 'ciudad de cantos, ciudad de santos' (city of stones, city of saints), and where St Teresa was born. Surrounded by perfectly preserved twelfth-century walls, it is Spain's highest provincial capital, standing at 1131m (3710ft), higher than Snowdon's peak in Wales. Here too I have experienced snow and sleet during early May! This overall view of the city is from the Cuatro Postes (Four Posts) on the Salamanca road. Loose peripheral treatment accentuates the main subject and its exposed situation. The new town can be seen down on the far side in the Adaja Valley.

Segovia and Avila, Castilla Y León.   Diary 7 May 1997

Avila, Castilla Y León.   pastel, 500x650mm

Sierra de Gredos.   Diary 4 June 2001

We head southwards towards Castilla La Mancha and Toledo over the Sierra de Gredos; an impressive, wild granite massif, with wonderful sculptured (through erosion) boulders, and umbrella pines, where you might be fortunate to see the Iberian Ibex.

I spent some time sketching and painting in Toledo during my first solo trip as well as taking in the El Greco museum and galleries, including Goya's work. Wonderful street cameos, café and restaurant subjects, the real hub of the city. The quite stupendously dramatic location of this wonderfully golden edifice is best seen from the Carretera de Circunvalación, with an even better, higher view from the terrace of the Parador. I hiked up to the heights well above these vantage points to find myself completely alone. The eroded stone is sculpted into strange shapes and particularly the interesting pile featured in both the sketch and painting. The 'snoopy-like' form is significant for the tablet at the top commemorates those who lost their lives during the Civil War. The view of the city surrounded by the Tajo ravine is spectacular and, in truth, I have yet to do it justice. The painting overleaf is pictorially interesting but lacks atmosphere. The sketch below is probably better!

Toledo, Castilla La Mancha.   Diary 8 May 1997

Toledo, Castilla La Mancha.
pastel, 600x800mm

Windmills of La Mancha, Consuegra, Toledo, Castilla La Mancha.
pastel, 450x800mm

Situated at the base of an isolated hill, east of the Montes de Toledo, and at the edge of the vast romantic plains of La Mancha, lies the small town of Consuegra. Surmounting the steep-sided hill are a group of windmills and a castle, the epitomy of the region which Cervantes' pen raised to the category of a transcendental literary image. These windmills and those at Campo Criptana, Alcázar de San Juan and Mota del Cuervo are the major groups which preside with majestic and loving countenance over the Quixotesque landscape, where a continuous spread of vineyards, olive groves and cereals are bisected by straight roads serving the small towns. A landscape full of atmosphere under a huge sky, and where the image of Don Quixote is forever present. The sky is usually clear and bright with a seemingly immeasurable infiniteness for most of the year.

The windmills of Consuegra are grouped mostly to one side of the castle and provide many striking compositions with the vast landscape far below, spreading outwards in an endless perspective of fields, lines of poplar and cypress trees to disappear in a violet-blue haze.

Perhaps the most striking view is from the south looking back to the castle over the windmills constructed at various levels along the ridge, and the town spread out below. The spot is very popular, particularly, it would seem, with Japanese tourists. Coaches bring visitors to a point below the last windmill and one is constantly surrounded by inquisitive onlookers. Most would appear to be on the 'Don Quixote Trail' and the buses do not, thankfully, linger for long. Nevertheless, this particular view is somewhat marred by vehicles at particular peak periods, one advantage painting has over the camera! One embarrassing moment was averted when, as I was approaching one of the windmills with another view in mind, I was surrounded by a gaggle of Japanese ladies, one of whom explained that their friend was 'Making herself comfortable', behind the building! Obviously no loo on the coach either!

The conditions can be changeable at springtime and this sketch (above right) from my diary during May 2001 painted from the

Consuegra, Castilla La Mancha.   Diary 2 May 2001

castle presents quite a different atmosphere to the two paintings produced from the southern end. The storm clouds could be seen approaching from way off until suddenly the wind reached a ferocity matched by the velocity of the near horizontal rain.

Consuegra, Toledo, Castilla La Mancha.   pastel, 325x500mm

Valdepeñas is usually our stop-over on the way down and back. The town is at the heart of the vast wine-producing area in southern Castilla La Mancha, supplying a substantial part of the country's wine output. The extreme climate (cold in winter, hot in summer and dry throughout the year) and the heavy clay soils give full-bodied wines which are very fruity and aromatic, and responsive to ageing in wood. The two main varieties of grapes used are Cencibel (Tempranillo) and Airén. As the diary notes mention, and one very good reason for stopping on our return journeys, we purchased two superb red wines last time; Pago Lucones Reserva and Vegaval Plata Reserva, both fermented and matured in the traditional manner.

As the sketch shows, the entrance to the town is lined on both sides of the road with huge, beautiful and traditional earthenware fermentation jars. The surrounding landscape is undulating with a few hills and an isolated windmill or two. Vibrant red clayey soil contrasts with the verdant (especially in spring) vines.

Valdepeñas Landscape, Castilla La Mancha.
pastel, 225x225mm

Monday 4th June.

Valdepeñas ...

Took on some wine before we left Valdepeñas - one very good reason why we planned a stop here. The vineyards around the town; the fresh young verdant leaves of the vines contrasting with the blood red soil, produce a superb wine. Protected on three sides by mountain ranges, the two main grape varieties of Cencibel (Tempranillo) and Airén produce the high quality red wines that have been made here for at least seven centuries. The three other grapes used are Cabernet Sauvignon, Garnacha and Macabeo. We bought some Pago Lucones Reserva, and Vegaval Plata Reserva from Bodegas Miguel Calatayud - both fermented and matured in the traditional manner - two of the very best houses - the wine is exceptional - which is the main thing. The business done, I produced this sketch of the impressive entrance to the town - the thoroughfare lined both sides by huge earthenware fermentation

Valdepeñas, Ciuadad Real, Castilla La Mancha.

Diary 4 June 2001

We continue further south along the N1V.E5 to the Sierra Morena, a mountain chain rich in minerals and covered by a scrub of oaks, lentisks (mastic trees) and arbutus (strawberry trees). This range marks the southern extreme of the Meseta, across which we have traversed, the immense Hèrcynian platform stretching all the way from the Cordillera Cantabrica in the north.

The 'Desfiladero de Despeñaperos', the pass over the Sierra Morena, is a large, spectacular and rugged cleft and beyond, stretched out endlessly in a shimmering violet-blue/green haze, lies the province of Jaen. The sun on the southern slopes of the mountains already feels warmer as the regiments of olive trees march away into the distance through the 'spiced blur of Andalucía'. The painting (right), completed entirely from memory, shows how the dual carriageway is separated, with the higher elevated route south enjoying the spectacular view.

Travelling on past whitewashed towns and villages with names such as Andujar, and Pedro Abad, the Moorish influence is quickly established. Past Córdoba with its outstanding Mezquita-Catedral, and Ecija, known as the frying-pan of Andalucía, lying in the Guadalquivir depression, we head towards Seville. I have only spent one day in the city, a break from painting in the vineyards of Jerez and the surrounding countryside, the main purpose of my stay.

'Desfiladero de Despeñaperos'.
pastel, 250x325mm

Vineyard, near Jerez de la Frontera.

Sandeman Vineyard, Jerez, Cadiz.

Diary 11 May 1997

Plaza de Toros de la Maestranza, Seville.

The campsite at Dos Hermanas on the south side is ideally positioned for a bus trip into the centre, and access to the landscape of Jerez. My day's break was not idly spent, a walk around the centre taking in the cathedral, and the Giralda, plus sketches. The bullring, facing the river, is a striking piece of architecture. Seville, whilst holding on to its traditions, has managed to keep up with the times. It is a wonderful place in which to stroll, pause and absorb the atmosphere and its many moods, whether it be one of the festivals or simply taking in the art of the tapeo. A much longer stay some time in the future is therefore a must.

One of my abiding memories of painting in the Jerez area south of Seville was coming across two 'brotherhoods' on their way to Rocío for the largest pilgrimage and most famous of all religious peregrinations in Spain. About 100 brotherhoods converge on this village in the Doñan, in carts, on horseback and vehicles, the women wear the rociero pleated skirt, and hats, whilst the men don a white shirt, black trousers and Córdoban sombrero. The sound of their singing, clapping, laughter and guitar playing is mesmeric, and the sight moving and colourful, which was briefly recorded by this small watercolour sketch.

'Brotherhood', converging on El Rocío. Watercolour sketch

The tent is at last extracted from the rear of the VW and erected for one of our principal sojourns in Andalucía, at Ronda due south-east of Seville and just 50km (31 miles) inland from the Costa del Sol. It could be 1000 miles away, for the town's geographical isolation and dramatic position above a deep ravine in the Serrania de Ronda are far removed from the concrete jungle on the coast. This Moorish settlement and immediate environs are a splendid source for subject matter, and a good base from which to explore the surrounding predominantly mountainous area. The wild and rugged landscape is occupied by the Pueblos Blancos de Andalucía (white villages of Andalucía), small towns and villages of breathtaking beauty. Their narrow, maze-like streets exude a Moorish air, lined by houses pierced by windows with ledges and large cornices which hold wrought iron bars; a substitution for the Moorish lattice box which allowed inhabitants to look out on to the street without being seen. If it were not for their whitewashed appearance, it would seem as though they had grown out of the very rock upon which they stand, in their harmonious and natural relationship with the landscape. As it is, however, they look as though they have been scattered from above to come to rest in a natural repose. I find the contrast between their 'contemporary' clean geometry and the soft verdant vegetation of an otherwise rugged landscape to be immensely stimulating and inspiring.

The area is one of the most beautiful and comparatively 'undiscovered' parts of the Iberian Peninsula and only recently have the minor roads been surfaced. In 1997 and during my journey to Casares, just 16kms (10 miles) back from the coast, our previous 1983 VW was restricted to 10 mph due to the state of the track.

I have explored and painted some beautiful locations from Ronda to the west as far as Arcos de la Frontera, northwards to Olvera, and south towards the coast as far as Casares. There are no coastal subjects in this book, for apart from greeting 'pupils' at Malaga Airport for tutoring sessions at Zuheros with 'Andalucían Adventures', and my brief romance with Sanlucar, I have yet to visit the shoreline. My work has been confined solely to inland Spain, 'the heart'.

The House of the Moorish King, Ronda, Malaga.
Diary 9 May 2001

looking up
to the Alhambra
Lunch in small
bar beside the
Darro & then the
climb up to Sacromonte.
Gypsy caves and
whitewashed dwellings
+ wonderful views of
the Alhambra - w/c sketch
from near the summit.
Met artist - a Granadian -
who invited me to his house/
cave/studio. Work inspired by
pueblo blancos - surrealistic & good.
Directed me to the highest
spot where the views of the
Albaicin, Alhambra and
Granada are superb. Took
spares of photographs &
the last study was thwarted
by running out of film!
With storm approaching I executed

The Alhambra
from Sacromonte.

The Alhambra from Sacromonte, Granada.   Diary 1 June 1997

Granada, at the northeastern foot of the Sierra Nevada, is where we pitch the tent again.

'Give him alms, woman, for there is no greater pain in life than being blind in Granada', which is to be found on a wall in the Alhambra, evokes the spirit and beauty of this city, its setting and monuments, the jewel of which is the Alhambra itself, one of the most magnificent creations to have been built by man.

The three Moorish hills of Sacromonte, Albaicín and Alhambra overlook the Christian city and the whole theatrical spectacle is backed by the impressive snow-capped Sierra Nevada.

The excellent bus system will take you from the campsite 'Sierra Nevada' into the centre, along the Via de Colón to the cathedral. From there everything is within walking distance. The Carrera del Darro, running alongside the Rio Darro between the Abaicín, Sacromonte, and the Alhambra, presents many cameos, with a small-scale village atmosphere enough to fill several sketchbooks. The Moorish Albaicín, rising through a maze of narrow alleyways, winding up through the palisades of cármenen (small villas) through delightful small squares and around tight corners, is Granada's most characteristic quarter. Requiring even more effort is the very steep Sacromonte hill, the gypsy troglodyte district. A lengthy climb to the top reveals a romantic and atmospheric view of mega proportions. I have made several studies from here, and it remains perhaps my

most favourite of haunts. I have never come across more than a handful of tourists who have made the effort in the heat, but the reward is well worth it. To pause on the way up beside a cave house and catch the refrain from a flamenco guitar drifting out through an open window is bewitchingly and hauntingly beautiful. By the time you reach the top and witness views such as those shown on pages 85 and 91, you are indeed in transcendental heaven.

The Alhambra is the supreme example of where the concepts of both fourteenth-century and the best of progressive modern architecture meet. Human scale is seen in both, areas where the strict overall economic use of materials is contrasted in relatively small intimate bursts with decoration and detail of the highest quality and sophistication. The harmony of a symmetry in the use of levels, and the way the garden and landscape are related to the building form, with water used to penetrate and link the interior with the exterior through the focus of the sky, light in the building, water and landscape; all of these considerations and architectural solutions add to the sense of modernity.

The beautiful Sierra de la Parapanda to the northwest is within easy reach and I have painted extensively there, as I have in and around Alhama de Granada to the southwest. Gaudix, the troglodyte town, to the north is perhaps the most fascinating of all with the sculptural chimney/vents and façades to the cave dwellings, and expensive cars parked outside the more prosperous areas, proving how practical they still are, and very paintable too!

Within the sketch, handwritten notes:

Houses and
conduit
alley.

Pampaneira.

Picnic lunch and then stroll
around the village -
sketches on previous two pages, followed by another watercolour baking.

down an alley with
conduit running in
the centre - the
sound and sight
of fresh clean
water on such a
hot day - most refresh-
ing - I couldn't have chosen
a better location!
Then I found this pleasing
composition - without
having to try too hard, for
subjects are to be dis-
-covered at every turn!
This little group
of Morisco houses
has a truly
sculptural feel!
Back to the site
stopping on the
way to look up
and across the
Poqueira gorge
for studies taking in the
three villages. Prepared
meal with Anne - who had
spent the day relaxing/reading.
Spaghetti - chorizo sausages, garlic,
onion, tomatos, aubergine, lettuce -
wine corked - otherwise good day!

Pampaneira, Las Alpujarras, Granada.   Diary 28 May 2001

Following the Christian reconquest of Granada in 1492, the Alpujarras became the final stronghold of the Nasrids.

On the southern slopes of the Sierra Nevada, after our stay in Granada we, too, head for this remarkable area straddling the provinces of Granada and Almería and lying between the Mulhacén to the north and the Sierra de la Contraviesa and Sierra de Gádor to the south. Small flat-roofed Morisco villages, clinging to rugged slopes, characterize the mountainous area with its fertile terraces and valleys, irrigated by the melting snows of the Sierra Nevada.

We base ourselves at Pitres in the Granada Alpujarras, the largest village of the seven settlements which make up the old Moorish territorial district known as the Taha, comprising Pitres, Capilerilla, Mecina, Mecinilla, Fondales, Ferreirola and Atalbéitar. The campsite, 'El Balcon de Pitres', just outside the village on the road to Pampaneira, is excellent with breathtaking views over the Trevélez Gorge to the Sierra de la Contraviesa, Sierra de Lújar and Sierra del Chaparral, a glorious landscape and the source of many of my paintings.

Not far (5kms) to the west through the Blood Ravine lies the Poqueira Ravine with the three villages of Pampaneira, Bubión and Capileira perched on the east side and rising up towards the Veleta. The irrigated terraced slopes with abundant vegetation, and flat-roofed Morisco houses, set in the contours and punctuated by the red roof tiles of the one church in each village, produce striking compositions. The villages are not so attractive when viewed from directly above, their flat roofs merging into one large blue/grey 'smudge' in the landscape. Generally, however, their individual cubes pierced with openings interlock both vertically and horizontally to create intricately interwoven ensembles set organically within the contours. Upon closer inspection the exposed chestnut beams and battens supporting the flat roof (terrao), a waterproof layer of bluish clay (launa), pierced by round tapered chimneys, all supported by lime-covered walls with iron grilles over windows set in deep reveals, present a living contemporary sculpture.

We explore similar villages further to the east, Trevélez, at 1600m (5248ft) the highest municipality in Spain, grouped like a pile of confetti beneath the Mulhacén. Juviles, Mecina-Bombarón, Yegen, where Gerald Brenan resided from 1920 to 1934, is a magical place set amongst vines, olives and, at 4000 feet overlooking the orange and lemon zone, it looks southwards from its airy position, towards the Sierra de la Contraviesa. Válor is next, then our route turns south at Mecina Alfahar before descending through orange and lemon groves, past barberry figs and century plants alongside the Rio Ugijar, through Ugijar and westwards to Yator on the lower northern slopes of the Sierra de la Contraviesa. The influence of the desert-like landscape of nearby Almería to the east spreads across this landscape; the hot earth colours ranging from dazzling searing white right through to the ochres to red. The distant slopes of the Mulhacén to the north cradle Yegen and the surrounding villages in a blue violet haze creating a landscape quite awesome in the scale of its spacial mood and atmosphere. From Cadiar to Los Tablones and Orgiva, the Guadalfeo presents a rugged remote landscape of great beauty and the inspiration for many of the paintings reproduced here.

boulder strewn river bed at the base of the narrow chasm-turned, ground, and behind, this breathtaking view of the western end of the village. Returned to hotel - Group thoroughly enjoyed their day in Córdoba. Dinner - superb paella - seconds!! + A Vera Lung!

Bailon Gorge, Zuheros, Córdoba.
Diary 17 May 2001

We leave the Alpujarras through Lanjarón overlooking the Valle de Lecrín, and known as the gateway to a region which has consumed me with its raw ruggedness on the one hand, and the breathtaking sophistication of its well-managed, irrigated and terraced landscape on the other. Human need for survival has, through integrity and skill, shaped it without destroying the essence of its natural beauty.

Our destination now is Zuheros in the Parque Natural de la Sierra Subbética, south of Córdoba, another region rich in glorious land-scapes, where the olive predominates. To reach there we travel west from Granada along the A92 as far as Estación de Salinas, before heading north to the Embalse de Iznájar at the southern fringe of the park, the town of Iznájar itself is magnificently located on the top of a peninsula that juts out into the embalse (reservoir). The mutli-coloured soil of the surrounding landscape is carpeted in olive groves.

The journey through the park along the minor roads reveals wonderful scenery. One moment we are down amongst the olives, the next high on a ridge with commanding views across marching armies of olive trees, all managed from the sparsely scattered farms, cortijos (homesteads) and lagares (olive estates). These dark gnarled limbs sporting rounded blue-green topknots encapsulate the mood, atmosphere and passion of the whole Mediterranean region. Whether observed from near or afar, its beauty is sublime and ageless.

I have already introduced you briefly to Zuheros on page 6. This unspoiled village is just south of Baena on the northern side of the Sierra Subbética. We have stayed here in the camper van, on the camping terrace overlooking the village, its myriad of roofs stretched out below reflecting light like an encrusted jewel. We have also stayed in the excellent Hotel Zuhayra whilst tutoring for tour company 'Andalucían Adventures'. It is the only hotel in the village and is run by two brothers, Carlos and José. Subjects abound here, both in and around the village and the surrounding olive-clad hills.

To the west of Zuheros are the Montilla-Moriles vineyards which produce the unfortified sherries much favoured by the Spanish where the 'wines' gain their high strength through the natural process of the fermentation of the Pedro Ximénez grape. Using Santaella as a base, the vineyards and villages of Montilla, Aguilar and Moriles are within easy reach. So too are the quite different agricultural settle-ments around Santaella itself where sunflowers, cereals and garlic are produced by villages possessing a frontier-like quality.

Windmills.
Campo de Criptana.
of the windmills there in rather dull weather. Continued my
on arrival at campsite, cooked meal & so to bed. The earth
if the weather improves tomorrow I should be in my element! Cuenca

Cuervo (Don Quixote country) where I made some studies
journey to Cuenca chased by following showers. Phoned Anne
is bright orange red in this area, contrasting with vivid greens—
looked quite stunning as I passed on my way to the site - only 5 km away!

Windmills, Campo de Criptana, Castilla La Mancha.
Diary 4 June 1997

Sadly we leave al-Andalus, as the region was known during the period of Moorish occupation, and for me an immensely rich source of inspiration. From the moment of emergence from the Desfiladero de Despeñaperos into this land of culture, tradition and richly varied landscape, it has been the quality of light which has constantly shaped the mood and atmosphere of the surroundings. Also by the people, so friendly, tactile and expressive in the way they pass their day, always orchestrated through discussion and music.

So, until the next time, we once more approach Valdepeñas, from the opposite direction, and for an overnight stop to take on wine! It was during a solo trip that my stay at the campsite here could have resulted in a shortened visit to Cuenca where we are headed now. Torrential overnight rain had reduced the site to a clayey quagmire.

Everyone was stuck, and being a bank holiday there was no tractor! However our first VW was rear-engined, and I managed very slowly to make my way up and out of the site, encouraged and cheered by the owners, and those resigned to an enforced delay, and others who were staying anyway! I felt both elated and somewhat like a rat jumping a sinking ship! As we shall discover later, Cuenca requires as much time as you can manage. Our journey down is retraced as far as Puento Lapice where we head due east through Alcazar de S. Juan to Campo de Criptana. There are vines in red earth and more windmills, this time spread out impressively along a hill top, but without a castle. We pass the last of the four principal windmill combinations at Mota del Cuervo, before heading up into mid-Castilla La Mancha to the Province of Cuenca, and the Serrania de Cuenca.

the form and general topography of the ravine. Whew! A quick snack and on to the spur which overlooks the Ciudad with the valley beyond and the Río Huécar below. The people who live in, and indeed those who built the houses overlooking the ravine must have had a good head for heights. The ochres of the cliff face, stone, and rendered walls capped by warm orange/red tiles contrast with the blue violets of the distant Altos de Cabrejas. This must be one of the most spec- tacular sights in Europe, and an area enjoyed to the full by the locals, who seem to be al- most constantly walking the ravine - some running. I stayed on, in the Ciudad, parking at the bottom next to the new theatre, and climbed up to the im- pressive footbridge spanning the ravine. Returning to the Plaza Mayor

Cuenca and the Hoz de Huécar, Castilla La Mancha.   Diary 6 June 1997

The Serranía de Cuenca is at the eastern end of the Meseta where the limestone massif has been eroded forming fantastic rock formations. The spectacularly sited old town of Cuenca is perched on a rock platform vertiginously high above the precipices of the Júcar and Huécar ravines. To add to the drama and through lack of ground space many of the houses were built tall and narrow.

The diary sketch of the old town was made perched right at the end of a spur overlooking the Hoz del Huécar. The view with the Parador, a converted monastery on the left, shows how the buildings seem to grow out of the limestone on which they were built. I found the splen- dour and magnificence of it all very moving. Here is where the work of nature and human endeavour combine to produce a homogenous delightful whole that is completely in repose and therefore just right!

One portion of this imposing edifice is recorded overleaf in my sketch of the Casas Colgadas (Hanging Houses). These are perhaps the most spectacular of the houses above the Huécar ravine. Built in the fourteenth century they literally appear to hang in the air, their balconies adding to the sense of vertigo, particularly for the occupants!

The streets winding up through the old town are narrow and full of character. At the upper end is situated the cathedral and Plaza Mayor, the meeting place where everything from politics, the arts, sport and just plain gossip is aired. It was here one evening that I witnessed the unfolding of the pure theatre and devotion of the pasos procession and the delightfully natural display of the evening paseo. Fairly exhausted after much walking, painting and sketching, I found an empty table in the square and ordered a meal. I was con- veniently positioned looking down towards the arched entrance to this meeting place, with the cathedral behind me.

The Spanish do not dine until 9.30pm onwards and so the surrounding tables were occupied by couples and whole families relaxing over an evening drink or two. The drama is documented in the diary excerpt reproduced below, the rapid sketch I made at the table before my meal captures something of the general atmosphere and ambience and perhaps a hint of what was later to unfold. The whole episode was a very fitting end to my productive and enjoyable stay in Cuenca.

Left: *Casas Colgades, Cuenca.* Diary 5 June 1997

Below: *Plaza Mayor, Cuenca.* Diary 6 June 1997

The Casas
Colgades.
Cuenca.

Plaza Mayor
Cuenca.

I found a table overlooking a colourful corner of the square and started to sketch. During the break for food (dinner out today), I watched a superb performance by the local policeman on traffic duty. Standing in the middle of the small space, and wearing sun glasses, his handset in one hand, a cigarette in the other, and with a whistle in his mouth he orchestrated everyone and everything. A family at the next table provided their tiny tots with buckets & spades with which they excavated round a nearby tree — supervised by Grandma who bellowed instructions, advice and admonishments from her seat at the table. Maria (the youngest) was the only name mentioned — probably her favourite — and possibly because she kept wandering off. Whilst producing this wk sketch the reason for the policeman's antics and the busy atmosphere became apparent. I had again "struck lucky" for into the square came a "Paso" procession — youngsters bearing a statue of the local saint, with also a band — most moving. I took photos — a very fitting end to a productive and enjoyable stay in Cuenca.

Olite, Navarra.

pastel, 250x325mm

The journey up through the Province of Guadalajara in northeastern La Mancha took me through vast areas of cereals contrasting with great swathes of vibrant red poppies. The Province of Soria in Castilla Y León presented a similar tapestry, the poppies joyously mingling with verdant cereals, whereas their cousins in Andalucía have long succumbed to the sickle in their favourite habitat twixt the olive and vine.

Beyond the town of Soria the minor C.115 dropped away from the Pto de Oncala and followed the course of the Rio Cidacos into La Rioja, through the most amazingly rugged scenery. The road dived through series upon series of clefts between opposing rocky spurs like the backs of dinosaurs. The resultant 'Z' bends slowed progress, but the visual experience was worth it. Leaving the Rio Cidacos to join the Rio Ebro at Calahorra I passed into Navarra and made the short haul up to the gothic town of Olite, the centre of the wine-growing area here. As can be seen from the painting, the town has all the appearance of a medieval city. The campsite is good, and the town, as well as being a good base for studying the surrounding area, is itself worthy of exploration. I was lucky enough to spend a Sunday in the Plaza Carlos III el Noble just sketching and people-watching. There I was in my shorts and sandals ensconced with my tapas and beer (it was hot) whilst everyone else was in their Sunday best, crossing the square from one bar/restaurant to another partaking in their traditional tapas rounds. I just observed and absorbed the ambience constantly fuelled by the chatter, which reverberated between all four sides of the square!

Vineyard, Rioja.
pastel, 400x500mm

The minor road north of the Rio Ebro and west of Olite winds through the small villages of Rioja Baja (Lower Rioja), Andosilla, Lodosa and Mendavia where more vegetables than vines are grown.

Lograno is the capital of this area, but beyond this busy town lies a concentration of vineyards running into and across Rioja Alta (Upper Rioja), which is reminiscent (to me at least) of Beaujolais, in the way every square-metre of land is fully put to use.

The acres and acres of vineyards around the villages of Biasteri, Labastida and San Vicente de La Sonsierra present a magnificent spectacle, a study in perspective with the verdant vines contrasting with flashes of poppies. The ripening cereals way beyond resonate with the complementary violet-blue haze of the far distant Cordillera Cantabrica. Haro, the capital of Rioja Alta, is a gem with a very good campsite. A stop-over here to take on some wine – with the space inside the VW at a premium during this, the latter stage of the journey.

Left: *Sonsierra, Rioja Alta.*   pastel, 400x500mm

Below: *Rioja Alta (Fonzaleche).*   Diary 9 June 1997

9th Monday.

Fonzaleche.
Rioja Alta.

yesterday.

Before leaving for the last leg of my journey I popped in to the centre of Haro to purchase some wine. The town is extremely characterful on the inside – & not too remarkable when seen from the outside – at least from the direction of Labastida – hence no study. I found what I wanted – some 1982 Marques de Murrieta, Castillo Ygay – superb wine and made from grapes (Tempranillo) grown on the largest single, self contained estate in Rioja – just north east of Logrono in Rioja Alta, where I passed through. Decided to take cross-country route - N 232 towards Santander.

Thursday 7th June.

View from our pitch - Santillana de Mar campsite.

Plenty of time before our sailing from Santander at 14.30 hrs so a lazy start to the day. Completed this sketch after breakfast - a typical "Green Spain" landscape quite different to those painted during the last few weeks! Coffee & fed up for a few moments before setting off for the Port. Straightforward drive-well signposted, and we were there before the ship - Val de Loire arrived. Snack, coffee and then back to the VW to witness the docking. Much activity of course, and time to quickly capture the last moments (sketch overleaf) before we joined the vehicle for the long process of embarkation. Had long conversation with local who came down to the quay to practise his English - which was excellent. Something of a problem whilst you are painting, but Anne helped out! What an interesting and pleasant man he was! Also besieged by pairs of schoolchildren

Santillana de Mar, Cantabria.
Diary 7 June 2001

The penultimate and very last day bring us back once again to the green-sided mountains and hills of Cantabria. La España Verde (Green Spain) is very different from everything we have seen throughout our journey through Iberia. The long descent to sea level winds through meadows dotted with whitewashed and natural stone farm buildings topped with red tiles, contrasting with the green pasture. The sketch (above) produced on the morning of our departure in 2002 from the campsite at Santillana de Mar is typical.

Finally the dock scene at Santander where in the same year I was constantly and delightfully questioned by groups of schoolchildren as part of their school project; 'What is your impression of Spain, Señor, and will you visit us again?' I think perhaps the contents of this book and the title of the sketch will give a firm indication of my reply!

Until the next time!

with oral questionnaires concerning our visit - in English of course - so my attempts at the sketch were quite punctuated. What an excellent idea though - and very good they all were too - and so polite - so indicative of their nation - their faith, ability to express their feelings, love of spectacle, immense pride, & current forward thinking.

Santander Dock.
Diary 7 June 2001

MAP OF THE JOURNEY

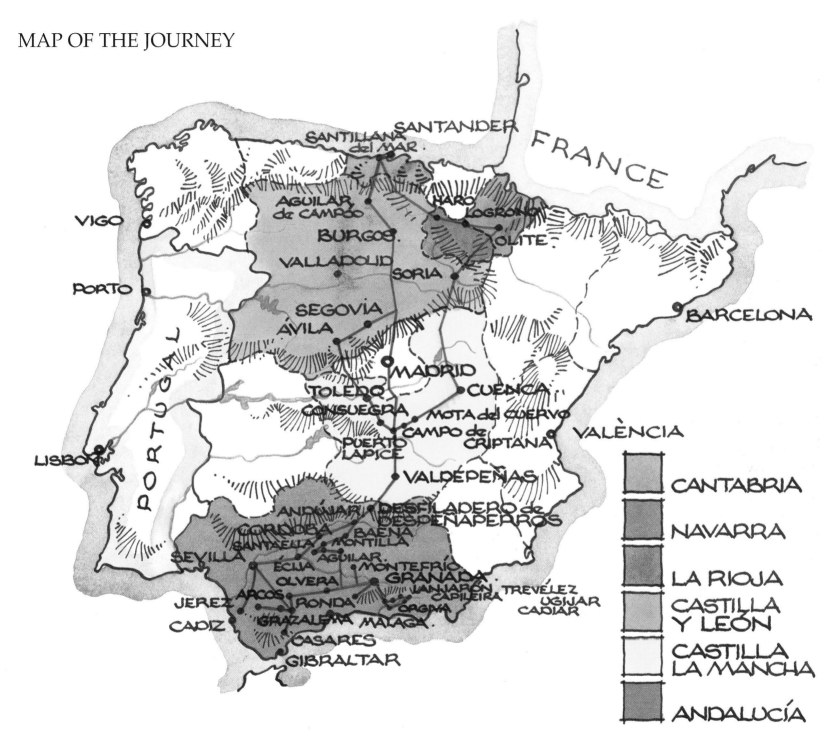

FRANCE

SANTANDER

SANTILLANA
del MAR

VIGO

HARO

AGUILAR
de CAMPOO

LOGROÑO

OLITE

BURGOS

VALLADOLID

PORTO

SORIA

BARCELONA

SEGOVIA

ÁVILA

PORTUGAL

MADRID

TOLEDO

CUENCA

CONSUEGRA

MOTA del CUERVO

CAMPO de
CRIPTANA

VALÈNCIA

PUERTO
LAPICE

LISBON

VALDEPEÑAS

DESFILADERO de
DESPEÑAPERROS

ANDÚJAR

CÓRDOBA

BAENA

SANTAELLA

MONTILLA

SEVILLA

ECIJA

AGUILAR

MONTEFRÍO

OLVERA

GRANADA

ARCOS

LANJARÓN

TREVÉLEZ

CAPILEIRA

UGIJAR
CADIAR

JEREZ

RONDA

ÓRGIVA

CÁDIZ

GRAZALEMA

MÁLAGA

CASARES

GIBRALTAR

CANTABRIA

NAVARRA

LA RIOJA

CASTILLA
Y LEÓN

CASTILLA
LA MANCHA

ANDALUCÍA

ANDALUCÍA – THE PAINTINGS

Feria, Zuheros, Sierra Subbética, Cordobesa, Córdoba.
pastel, 325x250mm

Spanish Broom and Almonds, Rio Trevélez, Las Alpujarras, Granada.
pastel, 325x250mm

Domecq Vineyard, Jerez, Cadiz.
pastel, 500x650mm

Cortijo, Jerez, Cadiz.
pastel, 250x325mm

Working from my base at the Dos Hermanas campsite outside Seville, the vineyards to the south surrounding Jerez de la Frontera, the heartland of sherry, provided plenty of inspiring and vibrant material. The light ochre, chalky albariza soil under the hot sun reflects light of piercing intensity. The perspective of the vines running over the gently undulating landscape accentuates the form in woven patterns of green, contrasted with the occasional patch of rich warmer-coloured soil and the red roofs of the Cortijos. Away from the vineyards, sunflowers bask beneath the vast blue sky stretching down to Sanlúcar de Barrameda where the moist Poniente wind blowing across the Coto Doñana produces the characteristic saltiness of the renowned dry Manzanilla sherry.

Vineyard, Jerez, Cadiz.
pastel, 500x650mm

Vineyard, Jerez, Cadiz.
pastel, 250x325mm

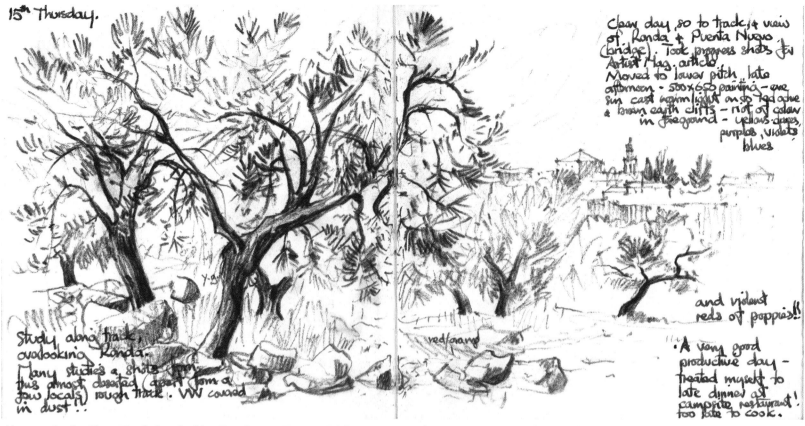

15th Thursday.

Study along track, overlooking Ronda. Many studies & shots from this almost deserted (apart from a few locals) rough track. VW covered in dust!!

Clear day so to track & view of Ronda & Puenta Nuevo (bridge). Took progress shots for Artist Mag. article. Moved to lower pitch, late afternoon - 500×650 painting - one sun cast warm light on so red ochre & brown earth cliffs - riot of colour in foreground - yellows, greens, purples, violets, blues

red/orange

and violent reds of poppies!!

A very good productive day - treated myself to late dinner at campsite restaurant! too late to cook.

Above: *Study Along Track Overlooking Ronda.* Diary 15 May 1997   Below: *Descansev en El Mercadillo and Puente Nuevo.* Diary 21 May 1997

A study from one of my many sorties along the track mentioned on page 15, and which have resulted in several plein air paintings, together with works completed from similar sketches. Ronda itself is full of cameos at every turn, and the Guadalevín Ravine separating La Ciudad (Old Town) from the more recent Mercadillo and traversed by the magnificent Puento Nuevo has a special quality of immense strength and depth manifestly emphasised by the purity of light and colour.

To the northwest lies Zahara de la Sierra, an absolute gem located on top of a hill and huddled beneath a huge rock capped by a castle. Its prominent position above the surrounding olive groves renders the almost sculptural composition a wonderful subject to paint – particularly looking into the sun and under evening light!

Crazalema to the west and nestling beneath the Peñon Grande in the Sierra de Grazalema on the way to Arcos de la Frontera flows like

a glacier between the craggy mountains, its setting and pueblo blanco townscape amongst the very best. Superb locally woven blankets, too!

Spring Flora, Ronda, Malaga.
pastel, 600x800mm

Puente Nuevo, Ronda, Malaga.
pastel, 325x250mm

Olive Grove Outside Ronda, Malaga.
pastel, 325x500mm

Tuesday 8th May

A walking day, following a visit to the
VW garage in Ronda - speedo & temp.
gauge + horn not working - to be
fixed on Thursday! We set out
towards Ronda, then turned
westwards along the track
leading to the Iglesia
Rupestre Mozarabe, the
cave church of Our
Lady of La Cabeza.
The ridgeway takes you
to the favourite place of
the poet Rilke and the
house where artist David
Bomburg lived whilst working
in and around Ronda.
The sense of open space
felt when arriving at the umbrella
pine clad ridge, is awe inspiring
This following a stroll through olive
groves covered with deep rich
red poppies & other flora - yellows
mauves, pinks, blues & sparkling white!
Ronda lay across the valley, perched on the cliff edge, the gorge breaking o
stillness - not a soul in sight - apart from the solitary worker with hoe! This sketch

Olive Grove and Poppies, Ronda, Malaga.

Diary 8 May 2001

to the open beneath the Puente Nuevo – birdsong breaking an almost eerie
on our way back thro' the olives. Pork, onion, potato, carrot & garlic fry – strawberries los Molino Valdes

Olive Grove below Ronda, Malaga.
pastel, 250x 325mm

The Tajo and Guadalevin Ravine, from the Puente Nuevo, Ronda, Malaga.
pastel, 500x650mm

The Hay Gatherers, Ronda, Malaga.
pastel, 250x325mm

Olives, Zahara de la Sierra, Cadiz.
pastel, 400x500mm

Zahara de la Sierra, Cadiz.
pastel, 325x500mm

Poppies, Zahara de la Sierra, Cadiz.
pastel, 250x325mm

Grazalema, Cadiz.
pastel, 400x500mm

Grazalema, Cadiz.
pastel, 325x250mm

Left: *Homeward Bound,*
Grazalema, Cadiz.
pastel, 225x175mm

Below: *Grazalema, Cadiz.*
Diary 19 May 1997

Grazalema.

stone somehow manage to provide some form
of anchor to hold the zigsaw together.
I have, at last got to grips with the
tonal subtleties of white architecture - my
contrasts in the first few paintings were
too pronounced and heavy - some
adjustments will be required in the
studio. Studies of Arcos have put
me on the right tack.
The white facades of course reflect all
surrounding colours and so there are
many subtleties here. Evening light -
towards sunset is when those plain
reflective cubes shimmer with warm colours
like some vast neutral stage set waiting
for stage lighting to accentuate the drama!
This is in contrast to the verdant foliage,
ochres, yellows reds, purple blue violets. Olive
groves, vegetables, wild flowers & sunflowers
surround Arcos & I think the latter will certainly feature
in a studio painting.

Midday Tapas, Grazalema, Cadiz.
pastel, 325x225mm

Arcos.

and studies from the south
and south east.
Perched on the headland above
the Rio Guadalete, this city
was among the most important
of Moslim Andalucía. No
sunflowers this time! Returned
along the N342 to Zahava de la
Sierra - superb view from hill to
the north east, where a dear old chap
was preparing soil amongst his olives and

vines - insisted on
taking me to his favourite
viewpoint - subject here! !
Anne meanwhile, looked through
Keeble Martin re flova. Great day -
returned to site - aubergine/cheese
based dish + Valdepeñas Reserve!

Arcos, Cadiz.

Diary 7 May 2001

The road west from Grazalema climbs up through the Sierra de Crazalema, a unique mountain wilderness where eagles (Bonellis', booted and golden), and vultures (Griffon and Egyptian) are common. They majestically cast their shadows across the van on our way up to the Los Alamillos Pass towards the village of Benamahoma and the small town of El Bosque. An area of outstanding wild beauty, it was once terrorised by ruthless bandits, and referred to in 1830 by Richard Ford as a 'robbers' lair'. 32 kilometres further on lies Arcos de la Frontera, the westernmost of the pueblo blancos, and one of the most beautiful in Andalucía. Perched magnificently on its great double crag of limestone, high above the Rio Guadalete, the dramatic location displays a shimmering cluster of white houses and sandstone churches clinging to the vertiginous rockface. Viewed from the surrounding countryside the spectacular ensemble continues to inspire me, and several paintings have resulted from my empathy with this beautiful place. The local landscape often conspires to project the dazzling spectacle to even greater heights, and I have painted the town across a blaze of colour with sunflowers, poppies, cork trees and barberry figs all in plentiful rich abundance.

Poppies, Arcos de la Frontera, Cadiz.
pastel, 500x650mm

Sunflowers and Cork Trees, Arcos de la Frontera, Cadiz.
pastel, 600x800mm

Poppies, Poppies, Arcos de la Frontera, Cadiz.
pastel, 600x800mm

Sunflowers below Arcos de la Frontera, Cadiz.
pastel, 600x800mm

Arcos de la Frontera (Sunset), Cadiz.
pastel, 500x650mm

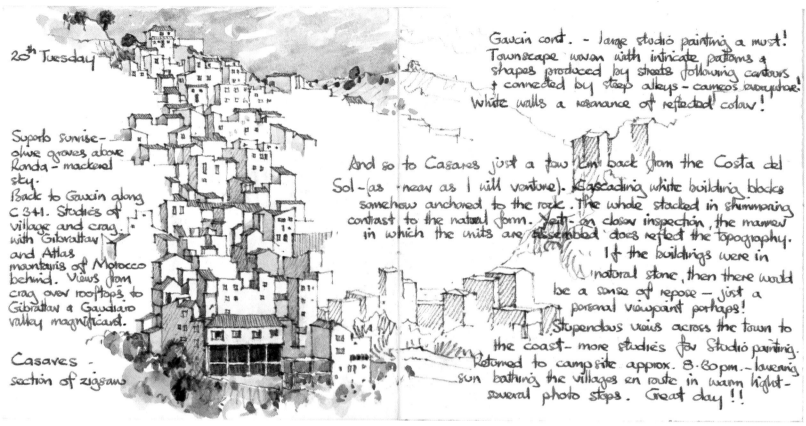

Casares, Malaga.
Diary May 1997

I have found much inspiration southwest from Ronda, along and adjacent to the C.341 coastal road, branching off as far as Casares just 16km back from the coast. This town is one of those places where the landscape and the urban setting coexist in such harmony, that it would be difficult to imagine one without the other. The organic structure of the town, its relationship with the natural contours, and the bowl-like spatial quality with extraordinary vistas down to the Straits of Gibraltar, provides subject matter of challenging complexity.

Back at the junction where I left the C.341, stands Gaucín, impressively sited in the Serranía de Ronda. From here the views down the Rio Guadiaro towards Gibraltar are even more spectacular, the rock rising in a distant violet-blue haze. On the return journey to Ronda the beautiful and gleaming villages of Benarrabá, Algatocin, Benalauria, Benadalid and Atajate fit the wild rugged terrain with white-gloved dexterity.

Casares, Malaga.
pastel, 325x250mm

Casares, Malaga.
pastel, 600x800mm

Casares, Malaga.
pastel, 500x650mm

Sunday 6th May.

Gaucín

Drove south-west
from Ronda along
the C.341 to Gaucín
and thence due south to
Casares. A repeat of my excursion
six years ago, but to my relief the road has been resurfaced with reconstruction
in parts, and the stretch from Algatocín to Gaucín particularly improved. My speed

Gaucín, Malaga.

Diary 6 May 2001

in our old (1983) VW camper
was restricted to 10-15 mph so
bad was the surface!
The sun tried hard to break
through the clouds as we
made our way through the
spectacularly beautiful
Serrania de Ronda.
The villages of Atajate
Benadalid, Algatocin
Gaucin and Casares
are jewels.
Their constructional
form follows the
natural contours -
the buildings welded
to the landscape.
Were it not for the white
shroud that cloaks these pueblo
blancos, their structural appearance,
would be truly organic. In truth they look
as though they have been scattered from above
rather than growing out of their foundations or the
rocks from whence they came. The secular buildings, usually
positioned at the top of the pile, do, in contrast, evolve naturally
through the expression of the natural materials upon which they were built-
the local stone. This view of Gaucin illustrates the point↓.
Casares is a joy - one of those places where the landscape and the urban

Gaucín, Malaga.
pastel, 400x800mm

Algatocin, Malaga.
pastel, 400x500mm

Atajate

church

Atajate, Malaga.

Diary 6 May 2001

setting coexist in such perfect harmony
that it would be difficult to imagine one
without the other. Several studies - streets
following the contours, with steep stepped
interconnecting alleys. Anne offered to
help one dear old chap making
his way to the top one such incline.
When she said she was
English he said Queen Victoria!
Studies of Algatocin, Benadalid on our way back and this
- sketch overlooking Atajate - a wonderful sweep of buildings with
acting as anchor: Tortilla a la Annie - superb meal - excellent full day!!!

Evening Light, Atajate, Malaga.
pastel, 250x325mm

Atajate, Malaga.
pastel, 500x650mm

Setenil de las Bodegas.
Diary 17 May 1997

Landscape near Olvera, Cadiz.
pastel, 250x325mm

At Setenil to the north of Ronda troglodyte dwellings are built into the rock which acts as a covering with the qualities of sculpture. These Cuevas del Sol (Caves of the Sun) and Cuevas de la Sombra (Caves of the Shade) form an impressive settlement built in between the rock formations on the steep hills enclosing the Rio Guadalporcún.

13km further north Olvera, with whitewashed houses surmounted by the castle keep and the Iglesia de la Encarnación, looks like a huge beached liner. The olive groves which the town surveys beneath its lofty perch, produce oil considered to be the finest in Spain. The landscape surrounding the town is rich in flora and fauna, and where tamed is covered in armies of 'marching' olive trees, forming complex patterns with their associated multi perspective. Their 'texture' over the folds, and the colour of the soil running from light-yellow ochre to deep-red ochre, all capped by an intense blue sky contrast sharply with the whitewashed town, which in turn absorbs and reflects these colours. With painting well under way (page 9) my work was curtailed by inclement weather suddenly sweeping in from behind me (Sierra de la Gazalema). The subject, full of colour and light, was finished in the studio.

Olvera, Cadiz.
pastel, 600x800mm

Olvera, Cadiz.
Diary 10 May 2001

Although this extract from my diaries was produced en route from Ronda to Zuheros in the Sierras Subbéticas, the N.342 through Olvera also leads to Granada, our next destination. I have also used the C.341 beside the Rio Guadalteba joining the same road at Campillos. On past the ancient town of Antequera, and the smaller Archidona, eastwards to Granada. On one working visit I was fortunate to be present during the religious festival of Corpus Christi. Thousands pack the Via de Colón for the procession of the Bigheads, and near to the campsite the Flamenco Feria pulsates day and night! In contrast I found complete isolation high above Sacromonte where I have spent many hours recording the breath-taking and spatial wonder before me. In truth I was directed to this particular spot by an artist, a Granadian who lives in a cave right at the very top. I was welcomed to his studio full of excellent paintings and sculptures all inspired by the local terrain and Moorish architecture.

The Alhambra and Albaicín from Sacromonte, Granada.
pastel, 600x800mm

Tuesday 22nd May.

Bad night! awakened to a
clear blue sky. We rested
during the morning - some correspondence
and sketching - then caught the No.3.
bus to the Grand Via de Colon and
alighted adjacent to the Cathedral. We made
our way via the Plaza Nueva - a couple of
studies - well proportioned buildings forming
backdrop to lively café scene.
Alongside the Rio Darro - more studies where
Moorish houses of the Albaicín flank the
many bridged river - the Alhambra towering
above the opposite bank.
We then climbed up the Cuesta del Chapiz
and along the Carril de las Tomases (sketch
opposite) cobbled alleys leading off, affording
delectable cameos in all directions! Screen
+ retaining walls sculpted to reveal glimpses
of the numerous small villas (cármenes), behind.
Arrived at the Mirador de San Nicolás to
witness once again the magnificent view of the
Alhambra (Annie for the first time). Even in the
tempered light from an overcast sky, the buildings
reflected a warm ochre glow, contrasting with
the verdant growth beneath. A snack outside the bar in the
square (painted last visit) and then a gradual descent along Isabel la Real to the

Carmen Carril de las Tamases, Albaicín, Granada.

Diary 22 May 2001

One of the many Cármenes along the Carril de las Tomases.

Plaza S. Miguel Bajo where we enjoyed pure theatre - conversations danced →

Restaurant, Plaza S. Miguel Bajo, Albaicín, Granada.
pastel, 175x175mm

Continuing the diary notes on previous page:

'… conversations danced across the delightful stage with participants – cats, dogs, children, grandparents, mothers, (fathers in bars), all orchestrated by the landlord of the bar opposite this restaurant, the fare and ambience of which we wearily and ultimately satisfyingly enjoyed.'

The Alhambra from the Mirador S. Nicolas, Granada.
pastel, 500x650mm

The Alhambra at Sunset, Granada.
watercolour, 470x595mm

The Alhambra from Sacromonte, Granada.
pastel, 400x800mm

Left: *Jardin del Partal, the Alhambra, Granada.* pastel, 175x175mm

Right: *Torre de las Damas, the Alhambra, Granada.* Diary 23 May 2001

Below: *'Wa-la ghaliba illa-Llah' ('There is no conqueror but God').* Diary 23 May 1997

Arabic inscription from the Salon de Embajadores, Casas Reales, taken from the Koran & tirelessly repeated in meticulous carvings. Wa-la ghaliba illa-Llah ('There is no Conqueror but God').

Elected to spend the day getting to grips with Granada and general topography - best achieved on foot - so I walked in to the centre from the camp site. Very busy main commercial and shopping street, Gran Via de Colon, forming spine. Stopped for coffee, toasted sandwich. Hordes on provisions for day on the Alhambra - & so to this most sensual piece of architecture. Intended to be a preliminary excursion, I stayed until approx 6.30pm. A few photos & rough sketches for the time being - the atmosphere and etheral quality somewhat ruined by

Jardines del Partal.

the accompanying hordes! The logistics & parking may prevent a completed

Torre de las Damas. Jardines del Partal . Alhambra.

orchestrated beneath the perfectly clear azure sky.

Then to the Palacios Nazaries where the decorative original-ality of the mocárabe vaults, domes, friezes and stuccowork combine with the effects of water and light - both of which are used as architectural features - to create an absolute jewel. The visual impact as one passes through small passages from the Cuarto Dorado to the Patio de los Arrayanes and the Patio de los Leones (sketch - previous page) is breathtaking, b. Views through delicately detailed windows to the Albaicín are spectacular.

Through to the Jardines del Partal and the graceful artes-onado portico and Torres de las Damas. We rested here, and I produced this sketch - bright, verdant spring colours set against, and harmonizing with the delicate design

The Arabic inscription above is from the Salon de Embajadores, Casas Reales, taken from the Koran, and endlessly repeated in meticulous ornamental stucco decoration. With its rhythmic repetition it is not intended to fire the imagination, but rather to liberate the onlooker from all pre-occupations of the mind. Specific ideas are not transmitted but, instead, a state of being, repose and inner rhythm.

Whilst I was drawing the inscription, I received a friendly tap on my shoulder. I turned to be confronted by a gentleman of obvious Moorish connections beaming from ear to ear, who informed me that instead of working my pen from left to right, I should have followed the Arabic practice of scribing from right to left!

Below the Alhambra, Granada.
pastel, 225x175mm

1st June.
Sunday.

I was awakened by the sounds from the Feria not far from the campsite. Multi vocal venderings belted through mega-speakers- the same as the five previous nights -except last night it went on all through the night. Fortunately I slept through it all. The final session is tonight so I may go along. In to the centre, this time by bus & a visit to the Cathedral-hugely impressive and not too ornate, apart from the chancel. Mass in progress. Then along to the Carrera del Darro, at the foot of the Albaicín. We sketch

Puente Espinosa.

Puente Espinosa, Granada.
Diary 1 June 1997

Los dos ríos de Granada
bajan de la nieve al trigo…

Granada's twin rivers tumble
down from the snow to the wheat…

Frederico García Lorca

The Carrera del Darro beside the Rio Darro (one of the two rivers, the other being the Rio Genil) lies between the Albaicín and the Alhambra hills, and is flanked by Moorish buildings exuding a village character.

Symmetry, the Alhambra, Granada.
pastel. 500x400mm

26th Monday.

Alhama de Granada.

Overcast again at campsite, but clouds high. Set off in direction of Alhama de Granada with view to painting the town overlooking the gorge. Studies of plair above Armilla, where cereals and poppi

Alhama de Granada, Granada.   Diary 26 May 1997

53km southwest of Granada the unsung gem of Alhama de Granada clings to a precipitous ledge overlooking the tajo (gorge) of the Rio Alhama. The character of the terrain changes en route to this fascinatingly beautiful place, from wide open plains, and then rolling olive-and-almond covered hills, to lakes cradled between mountains.

A spa town (Al Hamma in Arabic means 'hot springs') still used for that purpose, it is extremely well preserved. I have sketched in and around the old quarter and painted the gorge, but my everlasting memory will be the plein air work I completed overlooking the town and gorge from the south, under the late afternoon/evening sun (it was a very late return to the Sierra Nevada campsite at Granada that day!) There was a constant stream of locals taking the air on their circular walk, and their friendly manner was very warming, which delayed completion somewhat, but I shall never forget their genuine interest and knowledge of art, something which I found all over inland rural Spain.

Alhama de Granada, Granada.
pastel, 500x650mm

30th Friday.
Returned as anticipated to
the Parapanda area near
Montefrío. I must have become
accustomed to the pace of
life in Andalucia - in some
respects at least & on this I
will enlarge later - for in the
small village of Bracana (olive
grove studies) this morning
I waited 25 mins. in the one &
only shop for bread & water, +
3 bottles of Montilla Frío -the
best - unfortified, unlike those
of Jerez, whilst four elderly
señoras caught up with the
latest gossip & news. They were
also being served - of course.

The VW and I climbed
up towards Montefrío -
probably my favourite
town - not least for the
policeman who in front
of a large market crowd
on my last visit, and complete
with whistle fanfare, gave me
full VIP treatment. Seemingly to boost this

Parapanda Landscape, Montefrío, Granada.
Diary 30 May 1997

'Just before lunch (picnic) I executed the watercolour sketch of the
midday "white out" – just a little later actually. Not very much
colour apart from a supreme effort from the poppies! Very little mod-
elling due to diminutive shadows cast by overhead sun.'

Montefrío, Granada.
pastel, 500x650mm

Friday 25th May.

Back farewell to Granada under a clear blue sky. South to Las Alpujarras on the other side of the Sierra Nevada. As we approached Lanjarón we were confronted with a different landscape. Wild, rugged and mountainous, marked by winding gorges and watercourses fed by the melting snow high on the formidable Sierra. Picnic lunch - spit roasted chicken - and this sketch outside Lanjarón. On to Orgiva & north east to the villages of the Poqueira gorge, Pampaneira, Bubion and Capileira.

Lanjarón and Castle, Las Alpujarras, Granada.   Diary 25 May 2001

Lanjarón is the 'gateway' to Las Alpujarras stretching, according to Gerald Brenan 'like a balustrade all along a sloped escarpment'.

Although not apparent from this particular view looking at its western end, the buildings of this spa town are tightly spread along

Lanjarón and Castle.

Then higher along a heady twisting route to Pitres and the campsite of Balcon de Pitres at 4,000 ft. Absolute heaven - breathtaking views south, east and west. Variety of trees here - poplars, oak, chestnut, walnut, ash and a profusion of bushes - mock orange, jasmine, honeysuckle - nightingales by the score. Cooked Alpujarras pork, olive oil, garlic/herbs, onion potatos - beans, olives → mushrooms - washed down with Rosa - & so to bed!

the contours high above the Lecrin Valley. The landscape of the Morisco Alpujarra is 'wild, rugged and mountainous, marked by winding gorges and watercourses fed by the melting snow high on the Sierra Nevada'.

Pitres, La Taha, Granada.
Diary 26 May 2001

Our stay in 'La Taha' signalled an intense and concentrated period of work in the surrounding villages and delightful countryside. Below the campsite the clear light, so penetratingly vibrant at this high altitude, produced strong tonal and colour contrasts. Warm earth colours supporting fresh, verdant and colourful vegetation were gradually tempered through into the middle distance by the violet-blue haze softening the heavily cragged Trevélez Ravine. The Sierra de la Contraviesa and the Sierra de Lújar rise in a distant lighter violet-blue haze to provide a magnificent backdrop, with the depth of the pictorial perspective increased even further by the Sierra del Chaparral to the far southwest. Variations of this beautiful landscape, many of them recorded and painted during my 'hikes', are within walking distance of our base. Others were reached with our trusty VW 'studio', exploring in all directions. The results of my response to this wonderful region are reproduced on the following pages.

Bar and Jamine Alpujarreno, Pitres, Granada.
pastel, 225x175mm

Almonds above the Trevélez Ravine, Granada.
pastel, 500x400mm

Spanish Broom.
pastel, 325x250mm

Wednesday 30th May

Rio Trevélez ravine
and Sierra de Lújar.

exercise: I stopped as I

Rio Trevélez Ravine, Pitres, Granada

Diary 30 May 2001

Weather searingly
hot again! Anne
relaxed at the camp-
-site with a book while
I took a morning hike
down to Mecina Bond-
-ales. Several studies on
the way including this
sketch looking across the
Rio Trevélez ravine towards
Los Tablones and Puente Jübiley
with the Sierra de Lujar and
Sierra del Chaparral as backdrops.
Spanish broom contrasted with the pictorial perspect
-ive — blue/violet haze. Further down towards Mecina
through cherry orchards and almond groves — then the
sketch overleaf of Mecina and the Trevelez ravine behind.
The climb back from the ravine in the heat of the early afternoon was good
I came across the flora recorded on the following which provided several

Pampaneira, Bubión and Capileira, Granada.
pastel, 650x500mm

Old Beams, Pampaneira, Granada.
pastel, 325x250mm

Pampaneira, Granada.
watercolour, 310x230mm

Morisco Houses, Pampaneira, Granada.
pastel, 175x225mm

Villages of the Poqueira Valley, Granada.
pastel, 500x650mm

Bubión and Capileira, Granada.
pastel, 500x650mm

Trevélez, Granada.
pastel, 500x400mm

Yegen, Granada.
pastel, 250x325mm

Lemons near Ugijar, Granada.
pastel, 500x400mm

Over Lemons to Yegen, Granada.   pastel, 650x500mm

Towards Yegen, Granada.
pastel, 325x250mm

Cádiar, Granada.
pastel, 400x500mm

Almonds, Las Alpujarras, Granada.
pastel, 500x400mm

Rio Guadalfeo, Granada.
pastel, 500x400mm

Olives and Lemons, Orgiva, Granada.
pastel, 325x250mm

Sorvilán, La Contraviesa, Granada.
pastel, 500x650mm

From Bar Atayala, Zuheros, Córdoba.
Diary 17 May 2001

Zuheros, the village viewed from the Bailon Gorge on page 33, is surrounded on three sides by a sea of olives, the major produce of the Sierras Subbéticas. This typical Andalucían hill village and surrounding landscape has been the inspiration of many paintings.

Zuheros, Sierras Subbéticas, Córdoba.
pastel, 650x500mm

Zuheros from Terrace, Córdoba.

Diary 15 May 2001

walked up, & it was
Ellie who jumped aboard
with the locals. The rest of
us made our way to the
terrace overlooking the
village, for a painting
session through to
5.30 pm. Splendid
views over the
rooftops with
olive groves
marching over the
the distant hills.
Study of local
cutting fodder on the
terrace!.. Session slightly
marred by brief drizzle - soon
cleared. Returned to hotel with full
complement - the wanderers joined the
afternoon session - short break - then tutoring/discussion
re pastels, grounds etc until dinner at 8.00 pm. Chat afterwards then bed - phew!.

Sunset, Zuheros, Córdoba.
pastel, 500x500mm

Olive Burning, Zuheros, Sierras Subbéticas, Córdoba.
pastel, 225x225mm

Friday 11th May.

Awoke to a clear blue sky, sound of birds, and the rising sun just highlighting the castle, church, and the buildings beneath - the rest in the shadow of the cliffs rising behind us - great start to the day!

Met John at the hotel for tour around possible sites for tutoring sessions, and to acquaint us with the environment. Then to the current groups location at the ruined farmhouse near Zagrilla - the venue for dinner, this evening - Zagrilla, not the farmhouse!

Wonderful spot with all manner of subject matter - distant Moorish watch towers, olive groves, mountains, farmhouses, villages, century plants and Barbary figs, poppies and all manner of flowers!

Picnic lunch, and then this sketch whilst the group were being tutored by Roger.

Then on to the village for dinner - great ambience - Danny a thesbian (Black & White Minstrels) delivering joke after joke, with other members of the group contributing too! Good day! Learning all the time A.A' method of working. Returned to V.W. on the hill - crash out!

Landscape near Zagrilla, Sierras Subbéticas, Córdoba.

Diary 11 May 2001

Landscape near
Zagrilla.

Sierras Subbéticas, Córdoba.
pastel, 500x650mm

Springtime, Andalucía (Sierras Subbéticas, Córdoba).
pastel, 325x500mm

Friday 1st June.

Montilla.

Today, one of the highlights of the trip - from a touristic point of view and also aesthetic - a visit to the bodegas of Alvear in Montilla - a repeat for self but a new experience for Anne! Following a drive along a much improved road (since 97) we entered Montilla, the

Montilla, Córdoba.
Diary 1 June 2001

Santaella lies approximately 40km south of Córdoba, surrounded by undulating countryside, supporting vegetables, cereals, sunflowers, garlic and olives. We use an excellent campsite here, both to recharge our batteries before the push northwards, and to paint the local landscape.

Montalbán de Córdoba nearby is like a 'frontier town', not at all touristy, and possessing an honest, earthy atmosphere. We visited the town during their 'Garlic Festival', resulting in the working diary extract on pages 136–37.

The Montilla-Moriles wine (sherry) region to the east, as well as producing a wonderful product, possesses some interesting towns and villages set romantically amongst vines and olives.

Sunrise, Montilla, Córdoba.
pastel, 250x325mm

Saturday 2nd June

Montalbán de Cordoba.

The furnace heat continues - 35° - 36° again! Up early to enjoy the coolness, and
A very characterful non touristy working (agriculture) village, Montalbán straddles
the Dutch family from "next door" at the campsite - had chat and coffee in the square -
and thankfully in the shade, I was besieged by children and adults curious to see what
was her keenness to point out the location of her flat featured in the sketch! Anne
were preparing for the festivities ahead. There was quite a lot of activity at the top

Montalbán de Córdoba, Córdoba.

Diary 2 June 2001

to set off for the nearby village of Montalbán de Cordoba for their garlic festival.
a hill overlooking sunflowers, olives, cereals & vegetables including of course, garlic. Met
before executing this sketch surrounded by locals. Sitting on my stool on the pavement,
this white headed Inglisi was up to! much jollity - one lady almost fell into my lap, such
meanwhile sat near to the memorial reading, and absorbing the ambience as people
of the street behind me, so when the sketch was completed, and we bade the onlookers

Market, Montalbán de Córdoba, Córdoba.
pastel, 225x225mm

Córdoba.
pastel, 250x325mm

Olive Tree and Poppies, Santaella, Córdoba.
pastel, 225x225mm

Bailarina Flamenco.
pastel, 225x175mm

Baena, Córdoba.
pastel, 500x650mm

Aguilar de la Frontera, Montilla-Moriles, Córdoba.
pastel, 325x500mm

Home for Siesta, Grazalema, Córdoba.
pastel, 325x250mm